Contents

Chapter 1
Seven Ancient Wonders of the World: Why?

About 2,500 years ago, a Greek historian called Herodotus stared in wonder at a gigantic stone structure. Each of its four triangular sides was more than 200 metres wide at the base. The sides met at a pointed top 147 metres high. The structure covered more than 5 hectares of land. Herodotus was amazed but deeply puzzled. How did humans build something so enormous?

Herodotus was at the Great Pyramid in Egypt. When he viewed it, the pyramid was already 2,000 years old. Today, more than 4,500 years after it was built, the Great Pyramid still stands, and people still stare in wonder.

FACT

"BCE" is short for "Before the Common Era". This means all of history before the year 1 CE.

The Great Pyramid is one of the Seven Wonders of the Ancient World. Find out about the Seven Wonders and why they are on this list.

Great Pyramid of Giza

Herodotus's influence

In some ways, the list of Seven Wonders began with Herodotus. In the 400s BCE, Herodotus travelled through many areas near the Mediterranean Sea. He did so to write the history of a war between Greece and Persia.

As Herodotus travelled, he also wrote about wonderful sites he visited, including the Great Pyramid and the walled city of Babylon. Herodotus's descriptions of those sites led other people to visit them.

Herodotus did not create the list of Seven Ancient Wonders. In fact, many of the Wonders were not built until centuries after he died. However, Herodotus's writings did encourage people to learn about and visit amazing sites built by humans.

Lists are made

By the 200s BCE, other writers had followed Herodotus's example and described amazing structures. At times writers mentioned or created lists of wonders. But over the years, most of those lists were lost. It is unclear which places were on the missing lists.

This map shows what Herodotus believed the world looked like in the 400s BCE.

In roughly 250 BCE, a writer called Philo of Byzantium described the Seven Wonders. His written list, or most of it, has survived. It might have included some of the wonders that were on the lost lists. Philo also offered ideas about how each Wonder was built. He encouraged people to visit the Wonders.

A Greek poet called Antipater also wrote a list. Antipater's list of Wonders was the same as Philo's. In some ways, Antipater seemed like a traveller who took the advice of other writers and visited the site of each Wonder. Antipater even had a favourite: the Temple of Artemis. However, some of the Wonders had already been destroyed even before Antipater was born.

Antipater's list of Wonders

- Walls of Babylon
- Hanging Gardens of Babylon
- The Statue of Zeus
- The Colossus of Rhodes
- The Pyramids of Egypt
- The Mausoleum at Halicarnassus
- The Temple of Artemis

The ruins of the Temple of Artemis are located in present-day Jordan.

More lists

The Seven Ancient Wonders that Philo and Antipater named are very close to the current list of Wonders. But getting to that final list was not easy. Over the centuries when Rome ruled the world, other lists included structures built by Romans, including the Ishtar Gate of Babylon and the Egyptian Labyrinth. Although each structure was indeed marvellous, the lists were different from those of Philo and Antipater.

It was not until the 1500s that the list of the Seven Wonders of the Ancient World was settled. It happened during the *Renaissance period*, a time when scholars studied ancient history, especially Greek and Roman history. Scholars studied old writings and learned about many things, including the Wonders.

Artists created paintings showing what they thought each Wonder looked like. From then on, the list of Seven Wonders of the Ancient World was set in stone.

An artist in the 1500s imagined that the Great Pyramid looked like this.

PIRAMIDES ÆGYPTI.

FACT

The Renaissance period lasted from the years 1300 to 1700.

Why seven?

There were many amazing sites in the ancient world. So why is the list limited to seven? Long before the list was made, seven was viewed as a special number. Why? One reason may be that ancient people could easily see seven large objects in the sky. They saw the Sun and Moon and the planets Mercury, Venus, Mars, Jupiter and Saturn. Those objects may have helped make the number seven important.

The number of Wonders was limited for another reason. Thousands of years ago, the people who called these structures Wonders could only travel in parts of the world near the Mediterranean Sea. This is where the Seven Wonders could be found. The travellers could not possibly know about other wonderful structures that might have stood in other parts of the world. This may also explain why only two of the Wonders are distant from Ancient Greece.

In ancient times, people could map out seven objects in the sky: the sun, the Moon and five planets.

Why wonders?

Writers first called these amazing structures *theamata*. This Greek word means "things to be seen" or "must-sees". Eventually, though, writers used the word *thaumata* to describe the Wonders. This means "things to be wondered at or admired".

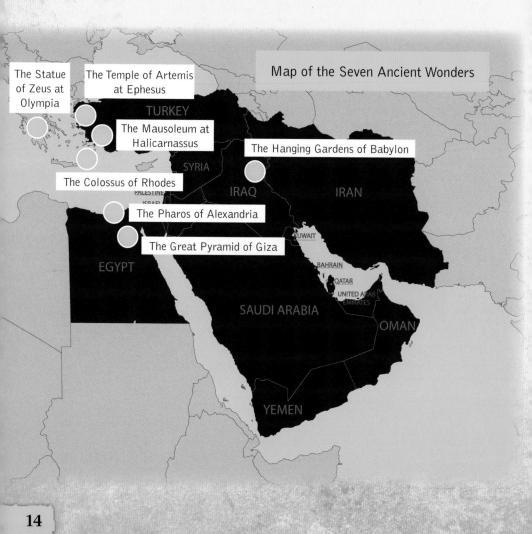

Map of the Seven Ancient Wonders

The Statue of Zeus at Olympia

The Temple of Artemis at Ephesus

The Mausoleum at Halicarnassus

The Hanging Gardens of Babylon

The Colossus of Rhodes

The Pharos of Alexandria

The Great Pyramid of Giza

TURKEY

SYRIA

IRAQ

IRAN

PALESTINE

ISRAEL

KUWAIT

BAHRAIN

QATAR

UNITED ARAB EMIRATES

EGYPT

SAUDI ARABIA

OMAN

YEMEN

Why ancient?

The word *ancient* means "old". This is why most of the Wonders no longer exist. They were built thousands of years ago. Over time, earthquakes or fires destroyed six of the Wonders. Yet there are details about how each Wonder looked and may have been built. Today, we still talk, write and read about the magnificent Seven. They still fill us with wonder.

THE SEVEN WONDERS OF THE ANCIENT WORLD

Wonder	Built (estimated)	Ancient name of location	Modern name of location
The Great Pyramid of Giza	2560 BCE	Egypt	Egypt
The Hanging Gardens of Babylon	600 BCE	Babylon	Iraq
The Statue of Zeus at Olympia	435 BCE	Olympia, Greece	Olympia, Greece
The Temple of Artemis at Ephesus	550–325 BCE	Ephesus, Ionia	Selcuk, Turkey
The Mausoleum at Halicarnassus	350 BCE	Caria	Bodrum, Turkey
The Colossus of Rhodes	280 BCE	Rhodes, Island of Rhodes	Rhodes, Island of Rhodes, Greece
The Pharos of Alexandria	280 BCE	Alexandria, Egypt	Alexandria, Egypt

Chapter 2
The Great Pyramid of Giza

The Great Pyramid of Giza was built in Egypt around 2560 BCE, nearly 4,500 years ago. It is the oldest of the Seven Ancient Wonders. It is also the only one that still exists today. For nearly 4,000 years, the Great Pyramid was the world's tallest structure. But in 1300, the old church tower of St Paul's Cathedral in London eclipsed this. It was taller than the Pyramid. Today, many structures are taller than the Great Pyramid.

Why is the Great Pyramid a Wonder?

This Pyramid has been called the most *colossal* building ever built. It was built with more than 2 million stone blocks. Each block weighed between 2,000 and 14,000 kilograms. The Pyramid's total weight is more than 5 million tonnes. The Pyramid was originally covered with limestone rock and was bright white and smooth.

The Great Pyramid is one of three large pyramids built at Giza. Giza is a broad area of land near the Nile River and high above the city of Cairo. All three pyramids are burial sites for kings, called *pharaohs*. The pharaoh was the most powerful person in Egypt.

This photo shows the three large pyramids at Giza. The tallest pyramid is the Great Pyramid.

FACT

Did you know that the Great Pyramid is also the largest tomb on Earth? It is the burial site for Khufu, a pharaoh of Egypt. Egyptians believed that the Great Pyramid would assist Khufu in his journey to the afterlife, a place of peace and delight.

How was the Great Pyramid built?

Building the Great Pyramid was no easy feat. The building began with a 10-year planning and preparation period. The plans had to be perfect to create such a large structure. The plans included details about its size, the kind of building materials that would be used and the number of workers needed. The plans also included details about secret rooms and entrances to keep away grave robbers and other unwanted visitors. The Pyramid had to protect both Khufu and the great treasures that would be buried with him.

When the planning had finished, it took roughly 20,000 workers as long as 20 years to build the Pyramid. For thousands of years after the Great Pyramid was built, people thought the workers were slaves. However, this is now considered untrue. Workers were paid with food and goods. They also worked because of a sense of duty to the pharaoh, to Egypt and to their religion.

FACT

Although Khufu's tomb is gigantic, the only known statue of him is tiny. It is only eight centimetres tall.

This illustration shows Pharaoh Khufu supervising the building of the Great Pyramid.

19

The Pyramid was built with huge stone blocks that were cut from *quarries*, or places where stone is dug from the ground. The blocks were loaded onto barges that travelled up the Nile River and through *canals*. At the building site, the massive stone blocks were unloaded and placed on rollers or sleds.

Men dragged each stone up ramps to where the stone was needed. How this was done is one of history's great mysteries. These ramps may have wrapped around the sides of the slowly growing Pyramid. Some experts think the ramps were actually inside the Pyramid.

The long planning period paid off because the building was constructed with extreme care. The huge stones fitted together perfectly, each side lining up exactly as the designers had plannned.

FACT

Granite blocks were used to build the burial room, or King's Chamber, in the Great Pyramid. The blocks weighed between 54 and 64 tonnes each!

This drawing shows men dragging a stone up a ramp during the construction of the Great Pyramid.

What happened to the Great Pyramid?

As careful as the building plans were, they were not perfect. Grave robbers had thousands of years to try to get into the Pyramid and the rooms where the pharaoh and his wealth were buried. Their efforts were successful. The body of the pharaoh has long been missing.

Eventually, even the limestone covering of the Pyramid was taken. The limestone is now part of many buildings throughout the city of Cairo. Yet the Pyramid still stands.

How do we know about the Great Pyramid?

Today, visitors can see what thousands of years of ageing, weather, pollution and other damage have done to the Great Pyamid. However, its size still fills visitors with amazement. Even at 4,500 years old, the Great Pyramid is in spectacular shape. After *all* those years, that is a great wonder!

A large statue of the Great Sphinx, which has the head of a human and the body of a lion, sits near the Great Pyramid.

A visit to Giza

Imagine the wondrous sights visitors saw after all three Giza pyramids were completed. The smooth, white limestone sides of the huge pyramids shone brightly in the sun. Mighty temples, smaller tombs and green gardens surrounded them. Water in nearby canals reflected views of the pyramids and temples.

Apart from the pyramids themselves, the most striking sight at Giza was the Sphinx. Although it seemed small next to the pyramids, the Sphinx was a huge statue of a sitting lion with the head of a man. Its body was 73 metres long, and its head was 20 metres high. Its face was the likeness of the pharaoh Khafre, Khufu's son. The Sphinx, with the strength of a lion and the brain of a man, was said to protect the ancient pyramids.

Chapter 3

The Hanging Gardens of Babylon

The Hanging Gardens of Babylon are one of the Seven Wonders of the World. They are a mystery and have been for thousands of years because the ruins cannot be found. So where are the remains of the Gardens? Did the Gardens really exist?

Why are the Hanging Gardens a Wonder?

Imagine this: In the middle of a large, ancient city there stands a huge structure of many levels. Each level has a wide balcony that wraps around the structure. Each balcony has beautiful plants and flowers of many colours draping over the sides. On the roof is a small, lovely forest of trees and colourful plants. Paths and benches wind through the forest. Even in the city's heat and sun, the forest always smells of fresh rain.

More than 2,500 years ago, a Babylonian king called Nebuchadnezzar might have built the Gardens for his wife to remind her of her distant homeland. It is a nice story, but is it true?

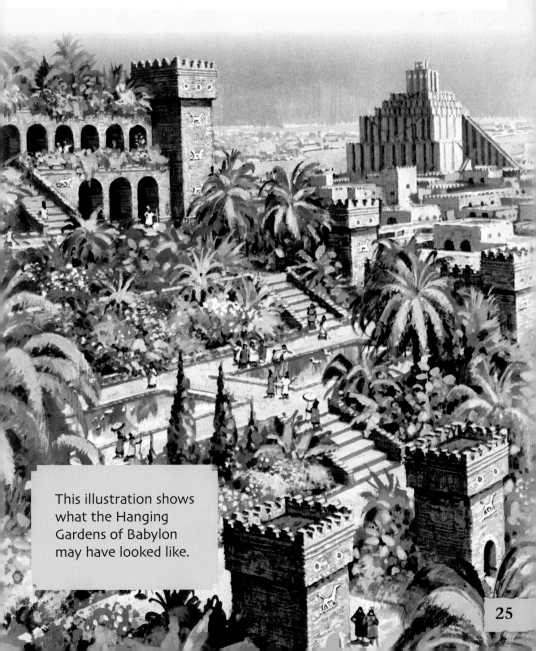

This illustration shows what the Hanging Gardens of Babylon may have looked like.

Why are the Hanging Gardens a mystery?

Many ancient writers described the Hanging Gardens. Some explained what the Gardens looked like, how they were built and how they were watered. These descriptions led to the Gardens' place on the list of Seven Wonders.

Yet other ancient writers never mentioned the Hanging Gardens at all. In King Nebuchadnezzar's time, the city of Babylon was well known for its beauty and for the thick walls that protected it. The walls were often discussed and were on some early lists of Wonders.

Herodotus visited Babylon at a time when the Hanging Gardens would have been there. He praised the beauty of the city and its walls. But he did not say a word about the Hanging Gardens.

For many centuries, there was no evidence to prove that the Hanging Gardens were real. There were not even hints of ruins. Until recently, the best chance of uncovering remains of the Hanging Gardens happened in the early 1900s. A German *archaeologist* was digging in Iraq where the city of Babylon once stood. He discovered the remains of ancient structures. He thought they might be the Hanging Gardens. What he found was important to understanding Ancient Babylon. But he did not find the Hanging Gardens.

This is a cylinder of written history of Nebuchadnezzar II's building activities from the 500s BCE.

What might have really happened?

In the 1990s, a British archaeologist studied ancient writings that discussed the Hanging Gardens. Others had studied these writings before, but this archaeologist found something new. She uncovered evidence that the Hanging Gardens may have been located in the ruins of the city of Nineveh in modern-day Iraq. Nineveh was about 480 kilometres away from Babylon. She found clues of an unusual garden and watering system in Nineveh. An Assyrian king is said to have built it. The archaeologist thinks this might have been the Hanging Gardens. Other scientists will work to prove or disprove this.

Will this Wonder come to be known as the Hanging Gardens of Nineveh? Or will the mystery of the Hanging Gardens never be truly solved?

This is what the Walls of Babylon may have looked like.

The Walls of Babylon

The Walls of Babylon protected the city's beauty, wealth and people. Ancient writers thought the walls should be one of the Seven Wonders. The walls' size and the way they were built help make them special.

They were built in the 500s BCE, nearly 2,500 years ago. An outer wall formed a square. Each side of the square was more than 19 kilometres long and 12 metres high. An inner wall was roughly 8 kilometres long on each side and 24 metres high. There was a water *moat* between the walls. Both walls were more than 6 metres thick.

The walls were made of baked mud bricks, not stone. This was a new building method. The walls had towers and gates. Some gates were beautifully decorated. The Walls of Babylon would have been a great addition to the list of Seven Wonders.

Chapter 4

The Statue of Zeus at Olympia

Does the word Olympia sound familiar? It should. In Ancient Greece, thousands of years ago, Olympia was where the Olympic games were held. The Olympics were part of a religious celebration honouring the god Zeus.

The Olympic games began more than 2,700 years ago, in 776 BCE. Yet it was not until more than 300 years later that a temple honouring Zeus was built. A Greek sculptor called Phidias was asked to build a statue of Zeus inside the temple.

Why is the Statue of Zeus a Wonder?

Phidias's statue showed Zeus sitting on a throne. Zeus was 12 metres high, as tall as a three-storey house. The statue filled a huge section of the temple from floor to ceiling. If Zeus came to life and stood up, his head would crash through the ceiling! Such a large body in a limited space made Zeus seem even more powerful.

Statue of Zeus at Olympia

How was the Statue of Zeus built?

In the 1950s, in the ruins of the temple, archaeologists found Phidias's workshop. The workshop had information about how he built the statue. There were notes, paints and samples of some building materials.

Phidias began the statue by carefully building a large wooden frame. The frame was then slowly covered with ivory and gold. Phidias shaped the ivory to show how powerful Zeus was. He also built a large reflecting pool inside the temple in front of Zeus. It caught sunlight from an opening above and lit up the statue.

What happened to the Statue of Zeus?

The Statue of Zeus had a long life – possibly 1,000 years. It remained in the temple until the late 300s. For most of that time, the Olympic games continued. In the year 391, the statue was moved to a palace in the city of Constantinople, in what is now Turkey. When a fire destroyed the palace in the 400s, the Statue of Zeus was destroyed with it.

The ruins of the Temple of Zeus still survive today.

How do we know about the Statue of Zeus?

There are written records of the statue and what it looked like. There are also records of other temple details. Zeus was holding an eagle in his hand, and images of animals and Greek gods were carved into his chair. Sadly, no paintings or drawings of the statue exist. There are ancient coins with images of the statue, but no one knows how correct those images are. All pictures of the statue that we see today are based on written descriptions.

The Olympic Games in Ancient Greece

Greek citizens came to the temple at Olympia to honour Zeus. One way they did this was through the Olympic games. Every four years, athletes from all over Greece came to Olympia to compete in the games. As many as 40,000 people watched the games.

At the start of the games, athletes made a promise to Zeus of fairness in competition. At the end of the games, athletes and viewers honoured Zeus at a closing ceremony in the temple. The huge Statue of Zeus was the centre of attention.

Chapter 5
The Temple of Artemis at Ephesus

Ephesus was a wealthy city in the country of Ionia, which is now part of Turkey. During the city's long history, five different temples were built honouring the Greek goddess Artemis. Each was always built on the same spot.

After the third temple was destroyed, a fourth one was built in 550 BC, nearly 2,400 years ago. This temple brought visitors from all over Greece. Money spent by visitors made the city of Ephesus even richer.

Why is the Temple of Artemis a Wonder?

The Temple of Artemis in Ephesus was built repeatedly because Artemis was important to the people of Ephesus. Eventually, the temple became one of the largest and most beautiful structures of the ancient world.

The temple was greatly praised for many reasons. It was made of marble. The outside may have been decorated with colourful art. Gold and silver decorations gleamed in and on the temple. Towering marble columns supported the roof and surrounded the central part of the temple. Inside, beautiful statues stood along the marble walls, including a tall statue of Artemis. The statue was visible throughout much of Ephesus. Passengers on ships entering Ephesus's port could see the statue through the temple's front opening.

Temple of Artemis

How was the Temple of Artemis built?

It was a great challenge to design and build the fourth temple. The temple's first *architect* almost gave up. Legend says that in a difficult moment, the goddess Artemis helped him. The giant temple was not finished in the architect's lifetime. It took 120 years and help from other architects to complete it.

Giant ramps were used to move marble blocks into place. The marble columns weighed about 40 tonnes each. They had to be moved 11 kilometres to the Temple. Moving them required an invention. The architect made huge wooden wheels that could be placed on each end of a column. The column could then be rolled to the building site.

This is an illustration of what the construction of the Temple of Artemis may have looked like.

What happened to the Temple of Artemis?

After all that hard work and effort, a man who wanted to be famous burned down the temple 2,700 years ago in 356 BCE. The fifth temple was built in a few decades. It was even larger than the fourth one. In the year 262, however, an enemy army once again destroyed the temple. The temple was not rebuilt.

How do we know about the Temple?

The Temple was the poet Antipater's favourite Ancient Wonder. Many other writers who visited the last two versions of the Temple left great written details about it. In 1869 archaeologists found buried ruins of the last temple – and evidence of the others built before it. They also discovered ruins of other ancient buildings nearby. Today, visitors can walk through the ancient history of Ephesus.

Looking under centuries of earth

In the mid-1800s, people wondered what J.T. Wood was doing. He was digging near to where the city of Ephesus once stood. Wood was an archaeologist who worked for the British Museum in London. Wood did not worry about what people thought, however. He just kept digging.

Wood discovered many ancient *artifacts*, including shattered sculptures, but none were those he was seeking. Finally, one day in 1869, he found a column of the Temple of Artemis. Over the years, Wood and other archaeologists uncovered much of the history of the famous temple.

J.T. Wood discovered
the Temple ruins.

Chapter 6

The Mausoleum at Halicarnassus

Like the Great Pyramid, the *Mausoleum* was a tomb. It was the final resting place for Mausolus, a king who ruled the ancient land of Caria. Today, this area is part of Turkey.

More than 2,300 years ago, during his rule in the 300s BCE, Mausolus made the city of Halicarnassus the capital of Caria. This city was a *seaport* on the Aegean Sea.

Mausolus was a clever ruler whose power grew during his lifetime. Before he died, Mausolus began planning his own tomb. After his death in 353 BCE, his wife, Artemisia II, became ruler. She asked the greatest Greek architects and artists for help finishing his tomb. The tomb became one of the Seven Ancient Wonders.

This drawing portrays the marble statue of Mausolus and his wife, Artemisia II, on top of the Mausoleum of Halicarnassus.

Why is the Mausoleum a Wonder?

Like most structures on the Ancient Wonders list, the Mausoleum was huge. It was built on a hill overlooking the city. It sat on a base that covered about 1,100 square metres and was about 32 metres high. On top of the base was a 7-metre pyramid. On top of the pyramid was a 6-metre sculpture of a chariot with four horses. The entire structure reached 45 metres into the sky. That's as tall as a 14-storey building.

The Mausoleum was very grand. Each of its four sides had fantastic sculptures. Some were of individual people. Some were of important moments in history. A long, wide stairway led to the tomb's entrance. Giant stone animals stood on both sides of the stairway. The white shining tomb could be seen from many kilometres away, including from far out at sea.

Mausoleum at Halicarnassus

How was the Mausoleum built?

The tomb was constructed with huge blocks and columns made of green lava or marble. These were cut from rock and shipped to Halicarnassus. As with other ancient buildings, it is unclear how these were lifted to great heights. A large machine, such as a crane, could have been used. Metal clamps and wood braces probably helped hold the blocks and columns in place. Building this giant tomb must have been dangerous work. The tomb was also well built. Except for the Great Pyramid, the Mausoleum lasted longer than any of the other Wonders.

What happened to the Mausoleum?

The Mausoleum stood for a long time. It was eventually damaged by a series of earthquakes. The amount of damage done is not clear. In the late 1400s, what remained of the Mausoleum was torn down. Its stones were used to build Bodrum Castle in Turkey. Green lava blocks from the Mausoleum are visible on outside sections of the castle.

How do we know about the Mausoleum?

The Mausoleum may have stood for as long as 2,000 years. Antipater claimed to have seen it, but he did not describe it in his writings. Pliny, a Roman writer, described it in the year 75. It is unclear whether he saw it in person or reported what others saw.

Experts have also learned much from those parts of the Mausoleum used to build Bodrum Castle. Archaeologists in the 1800s found many of the Mausoleum's parts at the original site. Some are on display in the British Museum in London. Some remain near where they were found. In the 1970s, Danish archaeologists learned more details about the Mausoleum and how it was built.

Today, the ancient city of Halicarnassus is the modern city of Bodrum, Turkey.

Chapter 7
The Colossus of Rhodes

The ancient city of Rhodes was on an island in the Aegean Sea. It was an important centre for sea trade. In 305 BCE, about 2,300 years ago, the country of Macedonia attacked Rhodes. The battle lasted a year but failed. In thanks, the people of Rhodes built a huge statue to honour the sun god Helios. It was called the Colossus of Rhodes. The Greek word *colossus* meant "statue".

Why is the Colossus a Wonder?

The Colossus was gigantic, standing 32 metres tall. It stood on a 15-metre marble base in the harbour of the city. No other ancient statue reached as high into the sky as the Colossus.

The towering statue was covered with bronze. The bronze made it shine brightly in the sunlight. It could be seen from a great distance on land and at sea.

How was the Colossus built?

When the army of Macedonia attacked Rhodes, it used huge war machines. One was a 37-metre tower. It was covered with iron plates and rolled on wheels. It was designed to break through the high walls protecting Rhodes.

When Macedonia could not defeat Rhodes, it left the war machines on the island. The people of Rhodes used those machines to build the Colossus. It's not clear how the people of Rhodes built the statue. They might have sold the machines to pay for the statue. Or they might have used the war machines as building material. Perhaps they did both.

The sculptor who led the building of the Colossus made the statue in three sections. He built up mounds of soil on each side of the statue. Workers stood on the mounds to set one section on another. It took 12 years to finish the work.

This portrait shows what the Colossus of Rhodes may have looked like.

What happened to the Colossus?

In the year 226 BCE, an earthquake knocked down the Colossus. The country of Egypt offered to rebuild the expensive statue. The people of Rhodes said no. They hoped to rebuild it themselves, but that did not happen.

In the 600s, the Colossus remains were shipped to Asia Minor, which is now part of Turkey. Some stories say that chunks of the statue were loaded on 900 camels and carried off for use as *scrap metal*.

How do we know about the Colossus?

The Colossus stood for about 60 years before the earthquake brought it down. Yet there is no doubt that the Colossus existed. One reason we know this is because the crumbled statue lay on the ground in big chunks for centuries. Visitors saw and wrote about what was left of the Wonder.

This photo shows the city of Rhodes as it looks today.

Did the Colossus stand over the harbour?

In the 1500s, artists made drawings of the Colossus standing with its legs *straddling* the entrance to the harbour in Rhodes. For centuries, people thought ships could sail between the legs of the statue. But that would have been impossible. The statue would have had to have been much taller than 34 metres for ships to pass under it. At the time the Colossus was built, it would have been impossible to make a statue that tall.

In fact, to stand at all, the Colossus had to be designed to stand up straight. Its legs would have been close together. Its arms might be straight over its head, but they could not reach out. If built any other way, the Colossus would have collapsed, even without an earthquake.

Chapter 8
The Pharos of Alexandria

In the 200s BCE, about 2,200 years ago, Alexandria, Egypt, was a new city on the Mediterranean Sea. It quickly grew into a busy seaport. Alexandria's ruler decided that a lighthouse should be built on Pharos Island near the harbour. The lighthouse would guide ships in the night or during storms.

When the lighthouse was finished 80 years later, it was gigantic. It was soon called the Pharos of Alexandria and was the last of the Ancient Wonders to be built.

Why was the Pharos a Wonder?

The Pharos was an amazing sight. It may have stood over 100 metres tall. For more than 1,500 years, the only structure taller was the Great Pyramid. Much of the lighthouse was covered with white marble. It gleamed in the sunlight. At night, the light of Pharos could be seen from over 40 kilometres away. It was a welcome sight for sailors and prevented shipwrecks.

The builders of the Pharos knew it would be worth visiting. They built steep stairways that allowed visitors to reach walkways many metres above the ground. From the walkways, the views of Alexandria and the sea were incredible.

This is an illustration of the Pharos of Alexandria.

How was the Pharos built?

The architect of the Pharos built the lighthouse in stages. First, a huge square base was built. Then, three sections were built on the base, one after the other. The first section had four sides. It was the tallest and broadest section. The middle section had eight sides and was covered with white marble. At the top of each section were walkways.

The third section had huge open windows. Marble columns held up its roof. A large fire burned in the open space. At night, this was the light of Pharos that guided sailors. Mirrors made the flames even brighter. During the day, smoke from the fire may have guided ships to the harbour. On the very top of the lighthouse stood a large statue, perhaps of an Egyptian ruler or a Greek god.

FACT

Some say the Pharos of Alexandria is the most practical structure of all the Seven Wonders. For centuries, its powerful beam of light helped protect and guide ships, sailors and passengers.

The city of Alexandria was named to honour Alexander the Great. He was a powerful leader who conquered much of the ancient world.

What happened to the Pharos?

The great lighthouse stood longer than any other Wonder except the Great Pyramid. During its lifetime, the Pharos survived earthquakes and ageing. At some point late in its life, it was no longer used as a lighthouse.

By the 1300s, the Pharos was in ruins. In the 1400s, a fort was built where the lighthouse had stood. Some of the old lighthouse stones were used in the building of the fort.

How do we know about the Pharos?

The Pharos lasted a long time. Many people saw and described the Pharos in drawings and writings. It was also shown on coins.

In 1994 large pieces of the lighthouse were found deep in the sea near the island of Pharos. Egypt plans to build an underwater museum. It will surround the ruins of the great lighthouse.

Who built the Pharos?

The architect of the Pharos was Sostratus. He proudly wanted his name carved on the lighthouse, but Alexandria's ruler wanted his own name on the lighthouse. Sostratus had no choice but to agree. On the outside of the Pharos, he carved the ruler's name on a large stone block. But it was not really stone. It was a plaster block. Over the years, the plaster wore away. Under the plaster on a real stone block, a new name was revealed. It said "Sostratus".

Alexandria, Egypt

Chapter 9

How the Wonders affect us today

The last Ancient Wonder was built 2,300 years ago. Yet the Wonders still have the world's attention. They have always inspired architects who design new structures. They still do.

The Wonders have also affected language. Thanks to the Wonders, words like *colossal* and *mausoleum* are used today.

The Wonders have always drawn visitors from all around the world. In fact, four million people visit the Great Pyramid every year. Two million visit Ephesus.

Wonderful buildings

Monuments around the world are modelled on the Ancient Wonders. For example, the sculptor who built the Statue of Liberty in New York studied the Colossus of Rhodes. The Statue of Liberty is even called "The New Colossus".

The Lincoln Memorial in Washington, D.C., is based on the Statue of Zeus at Olympia. Like Zeus, Abraham Lincoln sits in a temple.

This is a photo of The Shard in London.

At first, Lincoln's sculptor could not work out how to get enough light into the Memorial. He solved the problem by studying how Zeus's sculptor was able to get enough light into Zeus's temple.

The Pharos of Alexandria is not just a model for lighthouses but other buildings, too. The Shard, a skyscraper in London, is an example. At night, it even looks like a gigantic lighthouse.

The Mausoleum at Halicarnassus has inspired buildings such as The Shrine of Remembrance in Melbourne, Australia. Even the Hanging Gardens has inspired buildings like One Central Park in Sydney, Australia.

More Wonders

It would have been wonderful to visit some of these ancient sites, but tourists can see some new wonders today!

Taj Mahal

- Christ the Redeemer – a 30-metre tall statue in Brazil

- Great Wall of China – a more than 8,000-kilometre long ancient wall in China

- Machu Picchu – an ancient mountaintop village in Peru

- Petra, Jordan – an ancient Arab city in Jordan, known as the Lost City of Stone

- Pyramid at Chichen Itza – an ancient Mayan castle in Mexico

- Roman Colosseum – an ancient outdoor arena in Rome, Italy

- Taj Mahal – a mausoleum in India

TIMELINE

The Great Pyramid of Giza	2560 BCE
The Hanging Gardens of Babylon	600 BCE
The Statue of Zeus at Olympia	435 BCE
The Temple of Artemis at Ephesus	550–325 BCE
The Mausoleum at Halicarnassus	350 BCE
The Lost City of Stone in Petra	312 BCE (estimated)
The Colossus of Rhodes	280 BCE
The Pharos of Alexandria	280 BCE
The Great Wall of China	206 BCE
Roman Colosseum	70 CE
The Pyramid at Chichen Itza	600
Machu Picchu	1450 (estimated)
Taj Mahal	1648
Christ the Redeemer	1922

Glossary

archaeologist scientist who studies how people lived in the past

architect person who designs and draws plans for buildings, bridges and other building projects

artifact object made and used by people in the past

canal channel dug across land; canals connect bodies of water

colossal extremely large

granite igneous rock with visible crystals

mausoleum large building that holds tombs

moat deep, wide ditch dug around a castle, fort or town and filled with water to prevent attacks

pharaoh king in Ancient Egypt

quarry place where stone or other minerals are dug from the ground

Renaissance period period of art and learning in Europe in the 1400s and 1500s

scrap metal metal saved from old cars or machines

seaport town or city with a harbour for ships

straddle sit or stand with one leg on either side

Index